I SEE
THE
PROMISED
LAND

ARTHUR FLOWERS
MANU CHITRAKAR
GUGLIELMO ROSSI

I would like to thank my mother, who passed on her love for the word, and Gita, Manu and Tara Books for the gig, I'm honored to be part of the moment, my mother would be proud of this one.

- Arthur Flowers

LORD LEGBA,
OPEN THIS GATE.

It is I, Rickydoc Trickmaster, ask that this gate be opened, this work be done. I am a Hoodoo Lord of the Delta and power is what I do.

I AM MYTHMAKER.

SIT DOWN WHY DON'T YOU. REST A SPELL. I, MY FRIEND, HAVE A STORY TO TELL.

I suspect you've heard the Martin Luther King story as commonly told, but this a telling replete with the Will of the Gods, with Fate and Destiny and The Human Condition -

WHAT WOULD A TALE BE WORTH WITHOUT THESE THINGS.

IT IS FITTING THAT THIS TALE STARTS

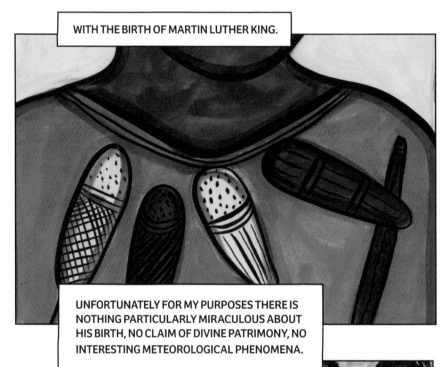

WITH THE BIRTH OF MARTIN LUTHER KING.

UNFORTUNATELY FOR MY PURPOSES THERE IS NOTHING PARTICULARLY MIRACULOUS ABOUT HIS BIRTH, NO CLAIM OF DIVINE PATRIMONY, NO INTERESTING METEOROLOGICAL PHENOMENA.

IT IS HOWEVER PERHAPS SIG-NIFICANT THAT HE IS THE SON,

GRANDSON AND

GREAT GRANDSON

OF SOUTHERN BLACK BAPTIST PREACHERS. THIS, IN FACT, CANNOT BE OVEREMPHASIZED.

1

He has an independent base. The Black Church one of the few forces in the black community not totally dependent on white patronage. Black preachers have always stood on the front lines of struggle and when it came time to move the people, King just turned his sermonizing skills into political oration.

RUN THOSE BIBLICAL CADENCES, THOSE PROMISELAND RIFFS, YOU HALFWAY THERE WITH BLACKFOLK. THEY WILL WORK W/YOU.

2

King what they call a raceman, from the progressive wing of the Southern Black bourgeoisie, folk for whom racial custodianship is a family tradition.

3

With a Doctorate in Systematic Theology,

KING SAW THE STRUGGLE AS AN INSTRUMENT OF MORAL IMPROVEMENT.

He had been influenced by Thoreau's Civil Disobedience and the example of Mahatma Gandhi to speculate a plan of nonviolent protest and activism. As a budding young theologian King expressed frustration with ministry that concern itself only with well being in the hereafter. King felt the well-apportioned ministry should also concern itself with well being in the world.

THE CASE CAN BE MADE THAT MARTIN LUTHER KING WAS BORN TO THE ROLE.

IT IS HIS FA.

NOW THAT DAHOME
- FATE, FREE WILL, A
QUITE SURE HOW TH
CLAIM WITH ALL MY
MARTIN LUTHER KIN
TEMPLE THAT NIGHT
PROMISELAND. IT WA
THE BALCONY OF TH
THAT NEXT MORNIN
FATED TO BE THE AN
TO US NOW. IT IS HIS

FA A FUNNY THING
THAT - I'M NOT
T WORK BUT I DO
OWER THAT IT WAS
'S FA TO BE IN THE
IE SAY HE SEEN THE
HIS FA TO BE ON
LORRAINE MOTEL
I CLAIM HE WAS
ESTRAL CALL HE IS
A.

NOW FA DON'T JUST DROP INTO YOUR LAP.

IT REQUIRE YOUR UNDIVIDED ATTENTION.

In his heart young King aspired to an academic position, a life of study and meditation, but he decided, emulating his own professors, that a pastorate would be an appropriate 1st step. How will you, young King, master Systematic Theology, if you have not been baptized in the field so to speak. So he take up the pastorate of the Dexter Baptist Church in Montgomery Alabama.

IN DOING SO HE STEP FORTHRIGHTLY ONTO THE HOODOO BOARD OF DESTINY.

Now, just cause you got the power doesn't necessarily mean you will be touched by the hard hand of destiny.

YOU DON'T BECOME TRUE FORCE UNLESS YOU CALLED UPON BY THE SPIRIT OF THE TIMES. THIS THEN IS THE CALL DESTINY FASHIONED FOR MARTIN LUTHER KING.

IT IS AS IF THE GODS, IN NEED OF AN INSTRUMENT, DECLARED THE BLACKS WERE TO BE THE DESPISED OF THE EARTH.

WE TALKING
SLAVERY NOW,

EUROPEANS IN THE WEST,

ARABS IN THE EAST,

AND, OF COURSE, AFRICAN
ON AFRICAN: WHERE TWO
BLACKS STAND, NONE
STAND TOGETHER.

THE BLACKS
ARE DECIMATED.

IT IS THE BLACKS OF WEST AFRICA THAT CONCERN US HERE,

CAPTURED,

ENSLAVED,

MANACLED AND MARCHED TO THE COAST,

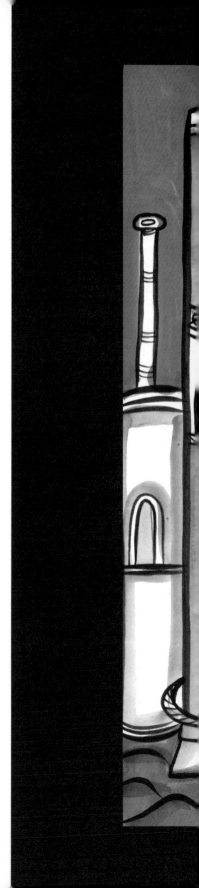

WAREHOUSED IN THE COASTAL CASTLES OF SHAME, GHANA'S CAPE COAST,

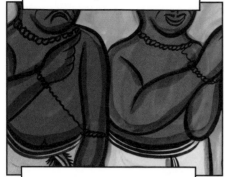

SENEGAL'S GOREE ISLAND,

THESE MUST BE EXPERIENCED TO BE BELIEVED, TO BE UNDERSTOOD, OUR ANCESTORS WAREHOUSED LIKE PRODUCE UNTIL THEY ARE STACKED ONTO SLAVESHIPS PACKFAT W/ HUMAN CARGO,

men, women and children basting in their own waste, sunk in despair and confusion -

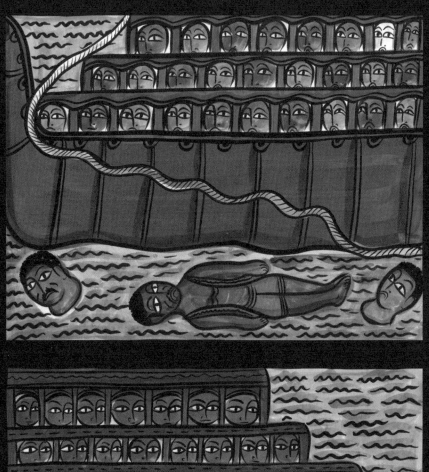

WHAT IS THIS PLACE,

WHO ARE THESE PEOPLE,

WHAT HAS BECOME OF US
(THE MIDDLE PASSAGE
THAT'S WHAT) -

HOW MANY MILLION DEAD,

TOSSED OVERBOARD TO
FEED WILY SHARKS THAT
FOLLOW EACH SHIP,

HOW MANY LEAP OF
THEIR OWN ACCORD.

THEN, ARRIVAL IN THE AMERICAS,

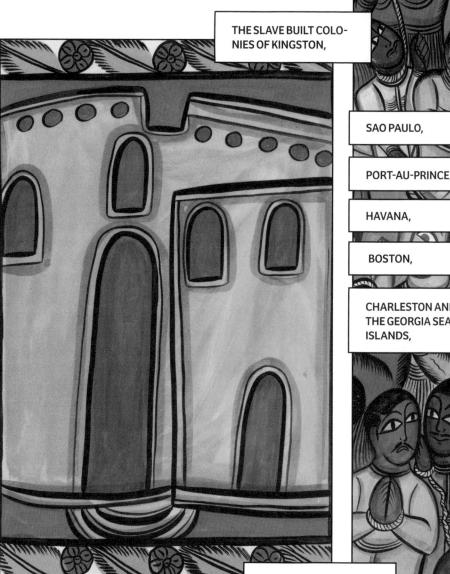

THE SLAVE BUILT COLONIES OF KINGSTON,

SAO PAULO,

PORT-AU-PRINCE,

HAVANA,

BOSTON,

CHARLESTON AND THE GEORGIA SEA ISLANDS,

THESE CAPITAL LINKS IN THE UNHOLY CHAINS OF SLAVERY.

This is the testing. For the Gods' purposes they must be stripped to the essence and what better scourge of souls than slavery.

BLACKS ARE TREATED LIKE SOME INHUMAN LIVESTOCK. WORKED TO DEATH. USED AS SEXUAL PLAY THINGS.

THEY ARE AT THE TOTAL DISCRETION OF THEIR MASTERS. IT IS LIFE AND DEATH ON A WHIM.

Some become runaways.

THIS IS THE WORLD
MARTIN LUTHER KING
WAS BORN INTO.

The apartheid South of Martin Luther King's day was little changed from the days of slavery.

TRUE,

slavery had been outlawed during
the Civil War by the Emancipation
Proclamation of 1863,

BUT THE KU KLUX KLAN,
RECONSTRUCTION AND THE
BLACK LAWS IMMEDIATELY
PUSH BLACKFOLK BACK
INTO THE QUASI SLAVERY
OF SHARECROPPING.

SHARECROPPING A
FEUDAL SYSTEM.

OLDSCHOOL. YOU
WORK THE LAND AND
YOU PAY OUT A PART
OF YOUR CROP.

But by the time settling up
come round you owe the man
so much for this and that you
never get out from under and
you totally submissive,

YESSIR NOSIR
ALL THE TIME,

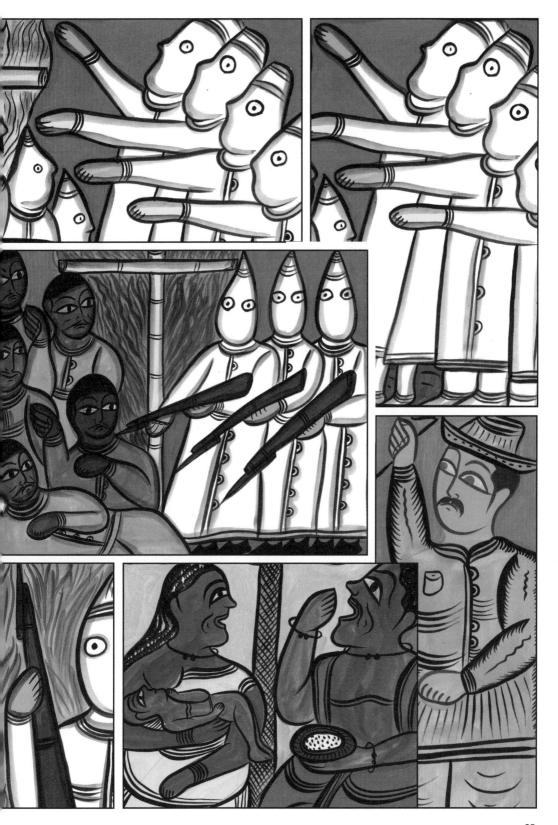

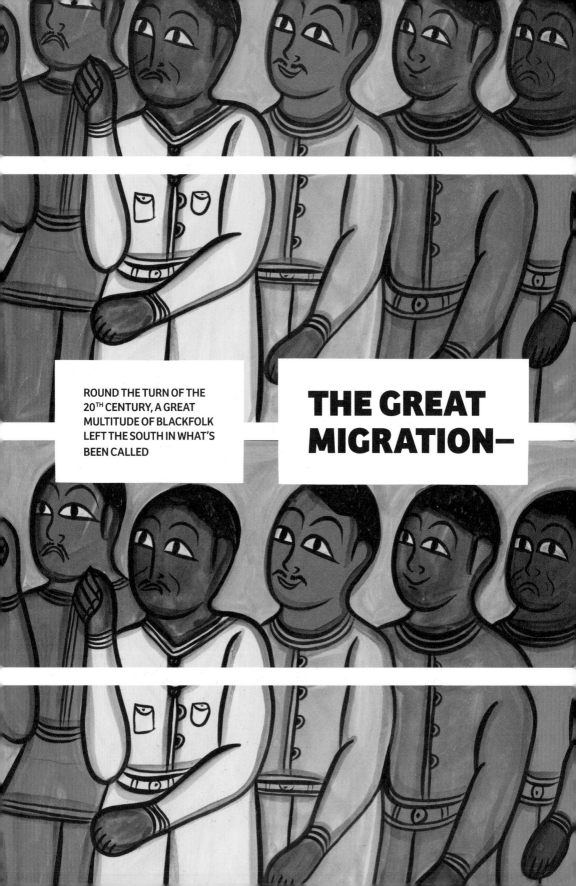

ROUND THE TURN OF THE 20TH CENTURY, A GREAT MULTITUDE OF BLACKFOLK LEFT THE SOUTH IN WHAT'S BEEN CALLED

THE GREAT MIGRATION—

a mass movement that turn a troubled rural folk into an

EQUALLY TROUBLED
URBAN FOLK.

So, now you got two contingents of blackfolk,

NORTH AND SOUTH.

NORTH, THE RACISM
MORE SUBTLE, DISCRIMI-
NATION MORE GRACEFUL,

BUT IN THE SOUTH IT IS
STRAIGHT OUT OPPRESSION.
BUCK NAKED APARTHEID.

Hard to explain to people what life was like in the apartheid South. Perhaps if you are an Untouchable of India, a black in the Sudan,

PERHAPS THEN
YOU KNOW.

YOU EXPECTED AT ALL TIMES TO DEFER TO WHITE FOLK, TO SIT IN THE BACK OF THE BUS, TO DRINK FROM THE COLORED WATER FOUNTAIN, TO STEP OFF THE SIDE-WALK IF WHITE FOLK COMING AT YOU.

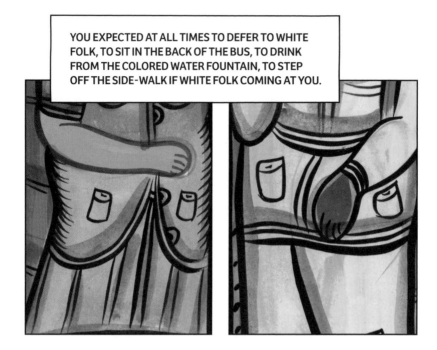

BLACKFOLK TREATED LIKE THEY NOT QUITE HUMAN.

CLOSE BUT NOT QUITE.

WORST THING, OF COURSE, IS THAT BLACKFOLK ACCEPT THIS TREATMENT.

BROUGHT UP IN THIS WORLD, REINFORCED BY ITS LAWS AND THE EVER PRESENT THREAT OF VIOLENCE,

THEY JUST DON'T KNOW NO BETTER.

BLACKS WHO DO CHALLENGE THE STATUS QUO

are often deprived of livelihood, homes and sometime their lives.

NIGHT RIDERS AND LYNCHINGS VERY PREVALENT IN THOSE TRANSITIONAL YEARS.

MEN, WOMEN AND
EVEN CHILDREN,

HUNG BY THE NECK
FROM TREES,

SOMETIME TORCHED ALIVE AND OFTEN MUTILATED BY CROWDS

THAT WOULD GATHER AROUND IN A PICNIC MODE,

CLAMORING FOR MEMENTOS LIKE EASILY REMOVED BODY PARTS.

This is the world into which
Martin Luther King is born.

THIS THE WORLD THAT PROVIDE THE CALL HE COME TO ANSWER.

Young Martin is expected,
of course, to follow in the au-
gust footsteps of his father,
his grandfather and his great
grandfather as pastor of
Ebenezer Baptist,

THE MONTGOMERY BUS BOYCOTT 1955:

The Touch of Destiny's Hand.

NOW, I SUSPECT YOU KNOW THE STORY, AT LEAST WHAT EVERYBODY ELSE KNOW.

MONTGOMERY ALABAMA, 1955,

THE RULE IS BLACKFOLK HAVE TO SIT IN THE BACK OF THE BUS, CAN'T SIT IN THE WHITE SECTION, HAVE TO STAND IN THE BLACK SECTION IF A WHITE PERSON WANT TO SIT.

But on this particular day, Sister Rosa Park's feet are tired and she don't feel like standing. So, she sat there on the hard rock of destiny and found it to her liking.

Local leader E.D. Nixon had been looking for a case he could use to challenge the bus laws and institute a direct action campaign. He recognize Sister Parks for the Blessing she is, somebody the community would defend and support. So. He call together the activist leaders of black Montgomery. They form the Montgomery Improvement Association, and

THE LEGENDARY MONTGOMERY BUS BOYCOTT IS ON.

NOW MARTIN LUTHER NEW TO MONTGOMERY. TOOK UP THE DEXTER CHURCH POST IN A BID TO ESCAPE THE LONG SHADOW OF DADDY KING AND HAD THROWN HIMSELF INTO MINISTERING HIS PASTORATE. THIS WHERE HE FORM HIS LIFELONG PARTNERSHIP WITH RALPH ABERNATHY. THEY BOTH MEMBERS OF THE ACTIVIST WING OF MONTGOMERY'S MINISTRY.

BUT HE ONLY BEEN THERE ABOUT A YEAR OR SO, SO WHEN TIME COME TO NOMINATE THE LEADERSHIP OF THE MONTGOMERY IMPROVEMENT ASSOCIATION, KING IS NOMINATED MOSTLY BECAUSE HE IS NOT ONE OF THE ENTRENCHED FACTIONS.

HE TAKE ON LEADERSHIP RELUCTANTLY.

HE FELT UNPREPARED, BUT WHO IS PREPARED WHEN FA CALL.

IT IS IN THE DOING THAT YOU GAIN THE GRACE.

The factions thought they had in King a malleable instrument that would take the heat if it all fell apart. It wasn't until he spoke at the 1st mass meeting with the community that the factions realize they had stumbled into the lap of destiny.

MLK A MACK.
A MASTER OF THE WORD.

AN ORATOR OF HISTOR-ICAL POWER, STATURE AND SIGNIFICANCE.

A MAN WITH A VISION.

"IF WE PROTEST COU
YET WITH DIGNITY A
WHEN THE HISTORY
IN THE FUTURE, SOM
TO SAY, 'THERE LIVE
OF BLACK PEOPLE, O
THE MORAL COURAG
FOR THEIR RIGHTS. A
INJECTED A NEW ME
VEINS OF HISTORY A

AGEOUSLY, AND

D CHRISTIAN LOVE,

OOKS ARE WRITTEN

BODY WILL HAVE

A RACE OF PEOPLE,

PEOPLE WHO HAD

TO STAND UP

D THEREBY THEY

NING INTO THE

D CIVILIZATION.'"

Some folk that was there that 1st
evening call it The Great Awakening.

He had not yet solidified his non-violence strategies. As all good things tend to do, that came out in the crucible of struggle, but you can see the seeds in his view of the Movement as a moral struggle and his evolving vision of the African American's role in America's destiny. And the destiny of the world too.

BOY GOT THAT LONGGAME VISION PUT EVERYTHING IN A STRATEGIC CONTEXT.

This is a good thing. For I would you my people be masters of strategy, the key that opens all locks. But I digress.

A GOOD STORY YOU GOT TO KEEP THE PIECES IN ORDER. ILLUMINATION IS A PROCESS AND THE LAYERS OF UNDERSTANDING MUST BE PRECISELY LAID.

THE BLACKFOLK OF BIRMINGHAM RESPOND

WITH AN UNPRECEDENTED BOYCOTT OF BUS SERVICES.

They set up car pools that defy tickets and all manner of harassment; both the hale and the canefolk walk the walk and defy all attempts to intimidate them.

The powers that be cooperate by refusing all redress.

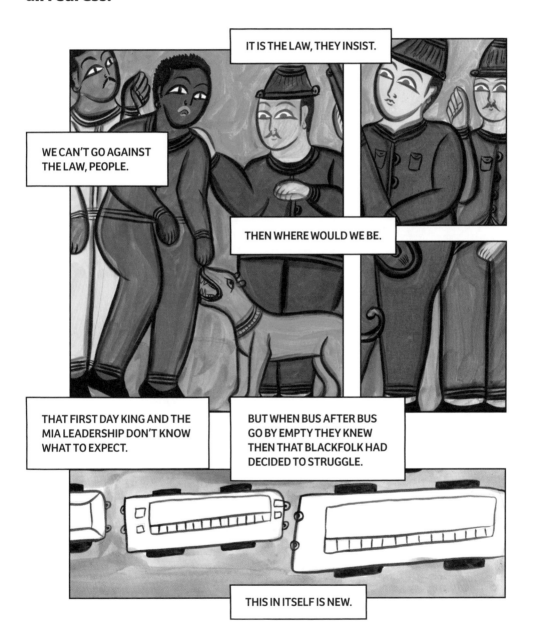

IT IS THE LAW, THEY INSIST.

WE CAN'T GO AGAINST THE LAW, PEOPLE.

THEN WHERE WOULD WE BE.

THAT FIRST DAY KING AND THE MIA LEADERSHIP DON'T KNOW WHAT TO EXPECT.

BUT WHEN BUS AFTER BUS GO BY EMPTY THEY KNEW THEN THAT BLACKFOLK HAD DECIDED TO STRUGGLE.

THIS IN ITSELF IS NEW.

The thing that most distress young King about southern apartheid is black acquiescence in their own oppression.

TOO MANY OF THEM ACCEPT INFERIORITY AS THEIR GIVEN PLACE.

BUT FOR 385 DAYS,

HOW DARE THEY CHALLENGE US. HOW DARE THEY CHALLENGE OUR WAY OF LIFE.

the blacks of Montgomery defy harassment, intimidation, bombs, and all manner of repression.

What was at first a joke to the powers that be became on some parts grudging respect, on some parts unreasoning anger.

Montgomery's intransigence convince the blacks, as Frederick Douglas once noted,

POWER CONCEDES NOTHING WITHOUT DEMAND.

They will have to make Montgomery give it up.

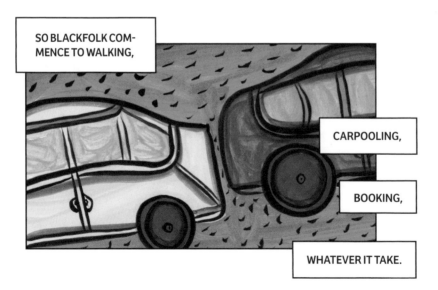

SO BLACKFOLK COMMENCE TO WALKING,

CARPOOLING,

BOOKING,

WHATEVER IT TAKE.

KING IS DELIGHTED. HE ASK ONE OLD WOMAN WALKING BY IF SHE WASNT TOO OLD FOR THIS, ASK HER IF HER FEET NOT TIRED.

MY FEET IS TIRED SHE SAY, BUT MY SOUL IS RESTED.

HE LIKE THAT.

HE LIKE THAT A LOT.

MADE HIS HEART FULL TO BURSTING.

MONTGOMERY GOT HOT ON HIM

ARRESTS,

DEATH THREATS,

BOMBINGS.

These threats reflect unsettling developments in American culture.

Brown vs. Board of Education had riled up oldschool whitefolk. Next thing they know they got blackfolk sitting in and marching and picketing and freedom riding and all manner of foolishness.

THE OLD SOUTH RESPOND BY CLOSING SCHOOLS AND SWIMMING POOLS,

AND WITH A REVIVAL OF THE KU KLUX KLAN, WHITE CITIZEN COUNCILS,

AND THE VIGILANTE VIOLENCE THAT HAD ALWAYS SERVED THEM SO WELL.

That little Emmet Till fellow, they say he whistled at a whitegirl, they necktied that boy w/barbed wire tied to a cotton gin and

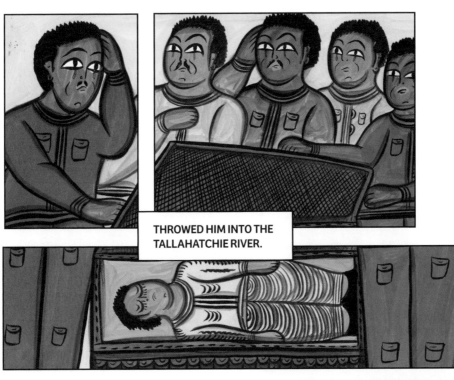

THROWED HIM INTO THE TALLAHATCHIE RIVER.

When King's house got bombed, friends and family back in Atlanta try to talk him out of it.

HE SAY I APPRECIATE YOUR CONCERN

BUT IT'S JUST TOO LATE.

At the mass meetings he kept the good colored folk of Montgomery fired up.

Note that move now; that redeem the soul of America bit. That little bit of ideological orchestration.

THIS WHAT MAKE MARTIN LUTHER KING SPECIAL.

HE SAYING THIS NOT JUST ABOUT US.

THIS ABOUT SAVING EVERYBODY.

KEEP AN EYE ON THIS, NOW.

EQUATING THE BLACK STRUGGLE WITH
THE STRUGGLE FOR HUMAN DIGNITY.

THIS IS WHERE
HE FIND HIS FA.

AFTER 385 DAYS OF STRUG-
GLE THE SUPREME COURT
RULED SEGREGATION IN
MONTGOMERY ILLEGAL
AND TO THE RELIEF OF THE
BUSINESS COMMUNITY THE
BUSES DESEGREGATED.
THE BLACKS COME BACK,

SITTING WHERE THEY PLEASE.

SCLC AND THE GREAT BLACK BOOK OF GENERATIONS

It is the Montgomery Bus Boycott that add Martin Luther King's name to the Great Black Book of Generations.

IT IS THE MONTGOMERY
CAMPAIGN ESTABLISH HIM
AS A LEADER, ESTABLISH HIS
NONVIOLENCE STRATEGY AS
ONE COLORED FOLK EMU-
LATE ALL OVER THE SOUTH.

FOR THESE ARE TUMULTUOUS
TIMES AND JUST RIGHT FOR
HIS BRAND OF NONVIOLENT
CIVIL DISOBEDIENCE.

BLACKS ALL OVER THE SOUTH STAND-
ING UPRIGHT. RAISING UP HEADS BENT
SO LONG THEY MOST FORGOT HOW.

THE JUBILANT VICTORS DECIDE THEY
NEED A MORE FORMAL ORGANIZATION.
ONE BASED ON THE BLACK CHURCH.

**They form the Southern
Christian Leadership Council
and set up office in Atlanta
with one employee, the
indomitable Ella Baker. Old-
line groups like the NAACP
and the Urban League are
wary of the newcomer.**

MARTIN ASSURES THEM THERE IS
MORE THAN ENOUGH STRUGGLE TO GO
AROUND. HE WOULD STEP ON NO TOES.

Basically this period of King's ministry consist of getting called into struggles to desegregate various cities across the South by local activists in need of King's high profile and strategic resources.

Like some Black Belt Pilgrimage, these cities have been entered into the Great Black Book of Generations:

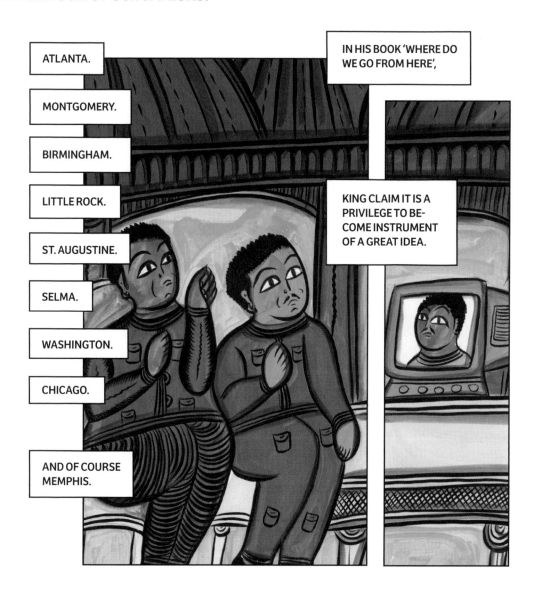

ATLANTA.

MONTGOMERY.

BIRMINGHAM.

LITTLE ROCK.

ST. AUGUSTINE.

SELMA.

WASHINGTON.

CHICAGO.

AND OF COURSE MEMPHIS.

IN HIS BOOK 'WHERE DO WE GO FROM HERE',

KING CLAIM IT IS A PRIVILEGE TO BECOME INSTRUMENT OF A GREAT IDEA.

He quote Toynbee's claim that the Negro will give Western Civilization the spiritual dynamic it so badly needs.

KING SAY HE HOPE THE SPIRITUAL POWER OF THE NEGRO CAN RADIATE OUT TO THE WORLD AND CHALLENGE THE NATIONS OF THE WORLD TO HIGHER GROUND.

THIS IS HEADY STUFF.

A CHOSEN PEOPLE SCENARIO TRYING TO AVOID THE CHOSEN PEOPLE SYNDROME BY ROOTING IT IN A VISION OF SERVICE.

This what bring King to a vision of black folk as a folk with a destiny.

THIS WHAT MOVE HIM TO THE PROPHETIC.

Ghana, he is Nkrumah's guest at his inauguration as president of the 1st African country to achieve independence. King realize now there is a world full of black people to serve.

India, he walk around New Delhi in a Gandhi cap, following in the footsteps of his idol, his mentor in struggle. He identify with the Untouchables and is impressed by India's affirmative action program, with Gandhi's attempt to give them dignity. Children of God indeed.

HE IS FURTHER REINFORCED IN HIS OWN BELIEF IN NONVIOLENCE AS A VIABLE STRATEGY.

"SIN
MOR
BEFC
NON
THE
AVA
PEOF
JUST
IN A
GANI
CERT
THAT
MOR
VERS
ARE
LAW

BEING IN INDIA, I AM
ONVINCED THAN EVER
THAT THE METHOD OF
OLENT RESISTANCE IS
ST POTENT WEAPON
BLE TO OPPRESSED
IN THEIR STRUGGLE FOR
AND HUMAN DIGNITY.
AL SENSE, MAHATMA
EMBODIED IN HIS LIFE
UNIVERSAL PRINCIPLES
RE INHERENT IN THE
STRUCTURE OF THE UNI-
AND THESE PRINCIPLES
INESCAPABLE AS THE
GRAVITATION."

He resolves upon re-
turning home to be
more like Gandhi. First
thing he do is set a day
aside for meditation
and reflection.

YOU KNOW ABOUT HOW
LONG THAT LAST.

THINGS TO DO.
PEOPLE TO SEE.

KING ACCEPT THAT HE
IS NOT THE MOST DISCI-
PLINED OF HOLYMEN.

Round about this time
he decide he need a
bigger stage. He leave
Montgomery and return
to Atlanta.

JUST IN TIME FOR HIS
NEXT BIG CHALLENGE.
ALBANY GEORGIA.

THE ALBANY MOVEMENT 1961

NOVEMBER OF 1961

THE ALBANY MOVEMENT IS FORMED BY LOCAL ACTIVISTS IN ALBANY GEORGIA.

1000s OF BLACKS ARE MOBILIZED IN A BROAD BASED ASSAULT ON SEGREGATION PRACTICES.

DECEMBER 1961, KING IS INVITED IN.

He decide he can spare a day for them but is arrested in a mass sweep and sentenced to jail. King refuses bail until city makes concessions he accept as a win but when Albany doesn't follow through on its promises he returns.

He is arrested again but understanding now the value of being incarcerated he once again refuses bail. The police chief, an equally perceptive fellow, surreptitiously pays his bail.

KING SAY HE'S BEEN THROWN OFF BUSES AND OUT OF LUNCH COUNTERS BUT THIS IS THE 1ST TIME HE'S EVER BEEN THROWN OUT OF JAIL.

After almost a year of struggle, dissension and a refusal by the powers that be to engage in mediaworthy violence the campaign's energy is sapped and SCLC withdraws in a defeat pregnant with lessons learned and new strategies.

CIVIL DISOBEDIENCE AND MARCHES HAVE BECOME THEIR PRIMARY INSTRUMENT

–strategy is to force confrontations with violent authorities and shame America by generating media coverage that force the government to act against the evident evils of southern apartheid.

The Southern position is that blacks are happy and comfortable with the system as it is and too many Americans believe this to be so.

MLK IS DETERMINED TO SHOW THE LIE OF THAT.

ALBANY IS COUNTED AS ONE OF HIS FAILURES, BUT FAILURES CAN BE USEFUL TOO.

Albany supply lessons King apply to Birmingham.

BIRMINGHAM: THE CHILDREN'S CRUSADE. 1963

It was Fred Shuttlesworth ask King into Birmingham. Spring of 1963 they commence a protest campaign. When Birmingham refuse to desegregate, SCLC implement Wyatt T. Walker's strategy of civil disobedience. Project C.

STRATEGY IS FILL THE JAILS AND PROVOKE THE AUTHORITIES INTO MEDIAWORTHY REPRESSION.

TELEVISION STILL A RELATIVELY NEW MEDIUM THEN

(APPARENTLY THE REVOLUTION WILL BE TELEVISED, YOUTUBED, FACEBOOKED, ET AL)

AND KING IS A PAST MASTER AT USING EVOLVING TECHNOLOGY AS STRATEGY.

HE IS ALSO ADEPT AT CLASSIC IDEOLOGICAL TECHNOLOGY

81

- arrested again and with a keen sense of the historical moment; King uses his time in jail to pen Letter From Birmingham Jail. It is a classic jailhouse manifesto, historical in its scope.

ALL HIS BOOKS WORTH READING. ONGOING ACCOUNT OF HIS STRA- TEGIC EVOLUTION.

Bull Connor's strategy is arrest them all and soon enough SCLC had run out of bodies.

SOMEBODY SUGGEST USING THE CHILDREN.

THIS IS A CONTROVER- SIAL SUGGESTION. THE DANGER SOME SAY.

ABOMINATION SAY OTHERS. NOT THE CHILDREN.

O THE HORROR.

BUT THE NEXT DAY
IT IS THE CHILDREN TAK-
ING TO THE STREETS OF
BIRMINGHAM.

MARCHING AND
SINGING THE
FREEDOM SONGS.

AIN'T GONNA LET NOBODY TURN ME A-ROUND. TURN ME AROUND.

The children of Birmingham. Marching on the frontlines.

IT IS A SIGHT TO
WARM THE SOUL.

AMERICA IS SHOCKED.
SHOCKED I TELL YOU.

This is more than the national consciousness (and local power brokers) can bear.

BIRMINGHAM CAPITULATES.

KING IS THE MAN AFTER BIR-MINGHAM. BLACK AMERICA'S ACKNOWLEDGED LEADER.

Many of King's demands are brought to fruition in the Civil Rights Act of 1964 and the Voting Rights Act of 1965.

WHEREVER HE GO HE CAUSE DOWNTRODDEN BLACK-FOLK TO BELIEVE IN THEMSELVES AND TAKE ACTION DESIGNED TO ALLEVIATE THEIR CONDITION,

NO MATTER THE DIFFICULTY, NO MATTER THE DANGER.

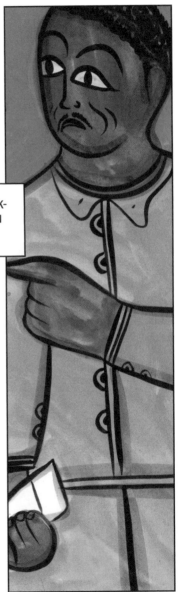

HE INSPIRE THEM LIKE NO OTHER SINCE OR BEFORE.

CAP IT ALL WITH THE MARCH ON WASHINGTON.

KING'S SHINING HOUR.

A COALITION OF CIVIL RIGHTS ORGANIZATIONS DECIDE TO MARCH ON WASHINGTON TO PUBLICIZE THE STRUGGLE AND DEMAND GOVERNMENT ACTION.

It is the largest gathering of protestors in the nation's history.

ORIGINALLY DESIGNED TO DIRECTLY CHALLENGE THE GOVERNMENT, IT IS DEMILITARIZED AFTER MARTIN MEETS WITH KENNEDY.

HE IS ACCUSED OF SELLING OUT. THIS HURT HIM. THIS HURT HIM BAD.

NOT ME HE PROTEST,

NOT ME.

But it all come through for him when he give them I Have a Dream.

A SPEECH THAT DEFINE THE MOMENT, AND FOR MANY, THE ERA.

KING IS AT THE TOP OF HIS GAME. THESE ARE THE YEARS OF HIS TRIUMPHS.

BIRMINGHAM,

THE MARCH ON WASHINGTON,

THE NOBEL PEACE PRIZE,

TIME'S MAN OF THE YEAR.

He on speaking terms with the powers that be and he basking in the adulation of the people. Got a loving wife and a growing family, got a vision –

ALL THE GOOD THINGS IN LIFE.

These of course are the years the Gods begin to extract the payment they always require of greatness.

Now that he The Man, new forces rise in the black community to challenge him as he had himself once challenged the old guard.

HIS CHALLENGE IS PERSONIFIED IN MALCOLM X, SELLING A VISION OF PRIDE AND VIGILANCE AND AN EYE FOR AN EYE VIOLENCE

THAT ANGRY BLACKFOLK FIND MIGHTY TEMPTING.

THE RISE OF MALCOLM REINFORCE KING'S DE-TERMINATION TO TRACK TO THE HIGHROAD. NOT ONLY DOES HE SINCERELY BELIEVE IN THE MORAL IMPERATIVE OF NONVIOLENCE,

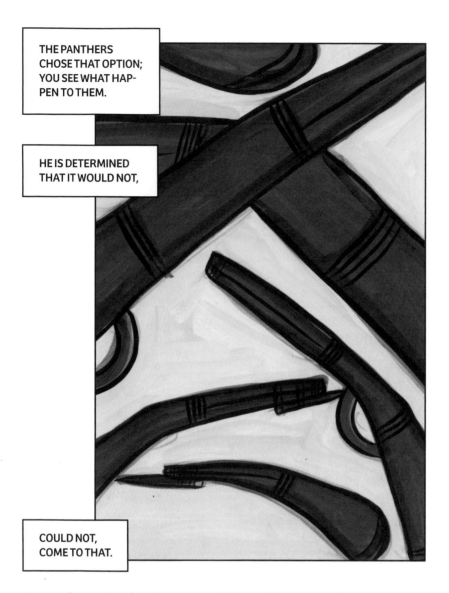

THE PANTHERS CHOSE THAT OPTION; YOU SEE WHAT HAPPEN TO THEM.

HE IS DETERMINED THAT IT WOULD NOT,

COULD NOT, COME TO THAT.

But where he had assured the old guard there were many roads to Timbuktu, now that he himself is challenged, he realize it's not that simple. To the old guard, new ways are often perceived not only as wrong, but dangerous.

KING'S PRIMARY CONCERN IS THAT BLACKPEOPLE NOT BECOME EMBITTERED BY STRUGGLE BUT ILLUMINATED.

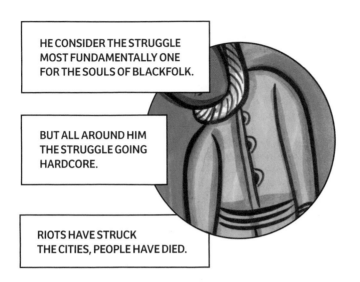

HE CONSIDER THE STRUGGLE
MOST FUNDAMENTALLY ONE
FOR THE SOULS OF BLACKFOLK.

BUT ALL AROUND HIM
THE STRUGGLE GOING
HARDCORE.

RIOTS HAVE STRUCK
THE CITIES, PEOPLE HAVE DIED.

In the philosophy of Malcolm, the Panthers, Black Power and the riots, Martin detect bitterness and frustration taking root in the African American soul.
The very thing he has tried to finesse.

GAINING THE NOBEL
PEACE PRIZE IS PERHAPS
THE PEAK OF HIS POWER,
THE YOUNGEST PERSON
EVER AWARDED IT.

HE IS HUMBLED BY THE EXPE-
RIENCE, BUT IT CAN'T HELP
BUT BROADEN HIS VISION OF
HIMSELF AND THE HISTORI-
CAL ROLE HE PLAYING.

It is at this point that he consciously couple the Black Struggle with the Struggle for Human Dignity.

"WE MUST FOREVER
STRUGGLE ON THE HI
AND DISCIPLINE."

WHAT HE SAYING HER
COME TO THE CROSS
THE HIGHROAD. ALWA
GREATER THAN YOU

But it is winning the Nobel Peace Prize that infuriate
his most implacable foe, J. Edgar Hoover of the FBI.
After his I Have A Dream Speech, Hoover call King

"THE MOST DANGERO
NEGRO LEADER IN TH
BETTER, "THAT GOD
PREACHER."

NDUCT OUR
IPLANE OF DIGNITY

IS WHENEVER YOU
ADS, ALWAYS TAKE
S STRIVE TO BE
E.

S AND EFFECTIVE
COUNTRY." EVEN
MNED NIGGER

NOW

PERSONALLY, I WOULDN'T MIND BEING CALLED THE MOST EFFECTIVE NEGRO LEADER IN THE COUNTRY,

BUT HOOVER CONSIDER THIS MORE OF AN INSULT THAN GODDAMN NIGGER PREACHER.

Using allegations of communist influence he convince AG Bobby Kennedy to authorize wiretaps on King.

This allegation of communist influence come from Southern barons convinced their Negroes are happy and satisfied Negroes.

Had to be outside agitators riling their Negroes up like this.

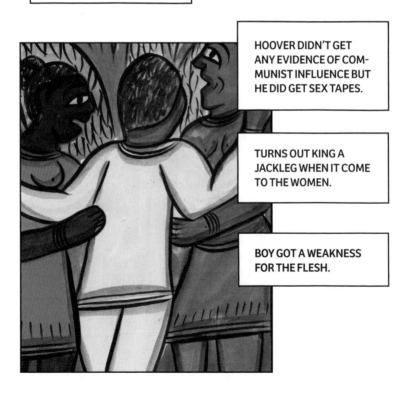

HOOVER DIDN'T GET ANY EVIDENCE OF COMMUNIST INFLUENCE BUT HE DID GET SEX TAPES.

TURNS OUT KING A JACKLEG WHEN IT COME TO THE WOMEN.

BOY GOT A WEAKNESS FOR THE FLESH.

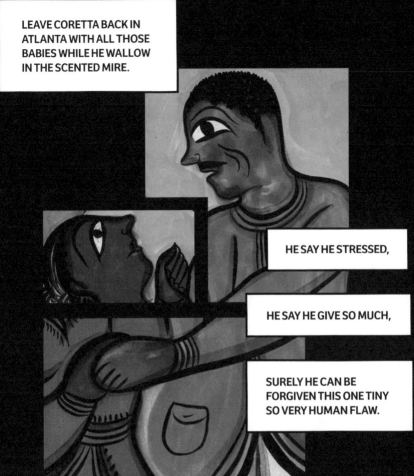

So, Hoover got all this juicy agonizing on tape and when King is chosen for the Nobel, Hoover send the tape to the King household with a note some contend encourage King to commit suicide.

Nonetheless, those early years, those early campaigns -nothing but victories-but that doesn't make for a very interesting story does it-its defeat that season the soul.

WELL, AT LEAST THE GODS ARE PLEASED. IN FACT THEY RATHER TICKLED.

THIS INSTRUMENT HAS BEEN ALL WE COULD ASK FOR, SAY THE GODS.

LET US NOW TEST HIM.

LET US SEND HIM TO ST. AUGUSTINE. LET US SEE WHAT HE MADE OF.

SELMA AND SAINT AUGUSTINE: THE STING OF DEFEAT

1964, local activists in St. Augustine, Florida begin a campaign of civil disobedience.

Same same Selma Dec '64, marchers obey an injunc-
tion that saps their momentum and again, defeat
and withdrawal. The powers that be have
learned how to counter his strategies.

MEANWHILE THE MOVEMENT HAS
GROWN MORE COMPLEX ON HIM.

IMPATIENT WITH THE PAS-
SIVITY OF NONVIOLENCE,
THE YOUNG TURKS HAVE
BEGUN TO TURN THEIR
BACKS ON KING AND HIS
NONVIOLENCE TOO.

This is exemplified
in his troubled rela-
tionship with SNCC.
The Student Nonviolent Coordinating
Committee had been founded with his
help and nurtured by SCLC in its infancy.
King is dismayed when they accuse him
of being an Uncle Tom.

(ACTUALLY UNCLE TOM HAS GOTTEN A
BAD RAP. CHECK THE TEXT, HE WASN'T
THAT BAD. DID WHAT HE COULD WITH
WHAT HE HAD. WASN'T NO GUNGA DIN.)

SOME IN SCLC BEGAN TO QUESTION ITS
RELIANCE ON MARCHES. VOTERS REG-
ISTRATION IS WHERE THE ACTION IS.

The Kennedy boys, hoping to blunt black
activism with electoral politics and pres-
sure the Southern barons, supporting it.
The people want it, SNCC riding it. Better
late than never, SCLC gets on board.

MISSISSIPPI FREEDOM SUMMER AND BLOODY SUNDAY: SELMA 1965

When SNCC decide to take voters registration activists into rural Mississippi, King and the SCLC advise against it,

> TOO DANGEROUS GOING OFF IN THOSE MISSISSIPPI BACKWOODS, THEY WARN.

SNCC, with the invincibility of youth, go into rural Mississippi anyway and the South respond with night riders and vigilante violence. Schwerner, Chaney and Goodman snatched out their cars and tossed into unmarked graves.

> BLACKS DARE REGISTER TO VOTE BOMBED, KILLED, FIRED, TOSSED OFF THE LAND.

> THE MISSISSIPPI FREEDOM SUMMER CAN BE CONSIDERED A SUCCESSFUL CAMPAIGN.

> O BUT THE COST.

IT ALL COME TO A HEAD ON BLOODY SUNDAY.

When SNCC and locals decide on a march from Selma to Montgomery, King advise against it and doesn't participate. Mob meet March at the Pettus Bridge. TV does it again, and the nation is riveted. How can this be.

King organize a new march but stops it at the Pettus Bridge. This infuriate SNCC and the locals. Once again King accused of being a sellout. The young Turks have taken to calling him "De Lawd", the saintly fellow from the movie, Green Pastures.

KING IS MORTALLY WOUNDED BY THIS.

AFTER ALL I'VE DONE HE PROTEST.

AFTER ALL I'VE GIVEN.

Stokely Carmichael replace James Farmer, as chair of SNCC. When James Meredith shot during his solitary March Against Fear, King, Stokely and others gather to continue it.

WHEN STOKELY CALL FOR BLACK POWER THE TENSIONS OF THE STRUGGLE COME TO A HEAD.

OLDSCHOOL AND NEW.

INTEGRATION OR SELF DETERMINATION.

WHICH DESTINY WILL IT BE.

STOKELY TELL KING, SORRY MAN,

I planned it to piggy-back off your high pro-file. King shrug it off.

I'VE BEEN USED BEFORE. ONE MORE TIME WON'T HURT.

OLD BOY TIRED.
OLD BOY WEARY.

WATTS and Newark got him reeling, burn baby burn, King feel the struggle slipping away from him. Driven by a need to regain lost ground, an expanding sense of his historical mission, the nagging call of Fa and a ministry that has begun to perceive poverty a violence as unjust as segregation,

KING MAKES DECISION TO NATIONALIZE THE STRUGGLE AND ATTACK THE CONDITION OF BLACKS IN THE NORTHERN GHETTOS.

LIKE SO MANY SOUTHERN BLACK MIGRANTS, KING DECIDE TO TAKE ON CHICAGO.

SWEET HOME CHICAGO; SORRY BUT I CAN'T TAKE YOU. 1966

To move on Chicago, SCLC ally with the Coordinating Council of Community Organization. King and Abernathy open the campaign with a little revolutionary theatre – moving their families into the Lawndale slum, nailing his manifesto to the doors of City Hall.

Test couples are sent out on housing discrimination missions, marches are sent into the ethnic enclaves of Chicago.

THIS BECOMES A REVELATION.

THE PASSION OF THE PROTESTORS SURPRISE THEM,

A HATRED, CLAIM ABERNATHY, WORSE THAN THAT OF THE SOUTH.

Between mob violence and Daley's machine politic, King is stymied in Chicago. Had that country boy spinning his wheels. After seeding Jessie Jackson and Operation Breadbasket, SCLC implement a strategic withdrawal, humbled and humiliated.

KING UNDER THE GUN NOW,

BLACK POWER ON ONE SIDE,

WHITE INTRANSIGENCE ON THE OTHER

AND A STRING OF CRIPPLING DEFEATS IN BETWEEN.

YOU CAN TELL HE FEELING HIS MORTALITY WHEN YOU LISTEN TO THE DRUMMAJOR SPEECH HE GAVE WHEN HE RETURN TO EBENEZER.

GOT UP TO THE PULPIT AND HE PAUSE SO LONG THE CONGREGATION BEGIN TO WONDER. GOT THEIR FULL ATTENTION WHEN HE FINALLY SPEAK.

SAY WHEN IT COME TI[ME]
TELL THE PREACHER N[OT]
HE TELL THEM DON'T [MENTION]
ON MY AWARDS, (WHI[CH HE WOULD]
LOVINGLY LIST). HE TE[LL THEM]
TO REMEMBER THAT [I]
TRIED TO FEED THE HU[NGRY,]
TO CLOTHE THE NAKE[D,]
BE RIGHT ON THE WAR [QUESTION,]
THEM MARTIN LUTHE[R KING]
AND SERVE HUMANIT[Y. A]
DRUMMAJOR. A DRUM[MAJOR]

TO GIVE HIS EULOGY,
T TO TALK TOO LONG.
STE YOUR TIME
HE THEN RATHER
THEM I WANT YOU
RTIN LUTHER KING
GRY. THAT I TRIED
THAT I TRIED TO
UESTION. TELL
ING TRIED TO LOVE
SAY THAT I WAS A
AJOR FOR JUSTICE.

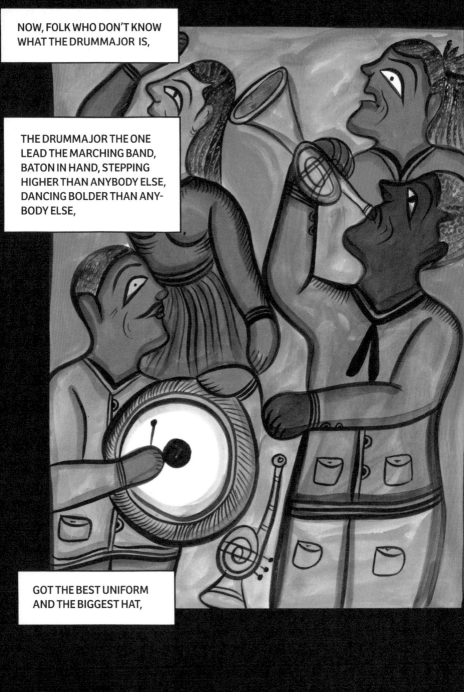

NOW WHAT HE CALLING THE WAR QUESTION,

THAT'S VIETNAM.

AFTER MUCH AGONIZING KING HAD FINALLY COME OUT AGAINST THE VIETNAM WAR

and for this he took much grief. Old allies from Roy Wilkins to LBJ turn on him and the once adoring media pillory him, liberals, conservatives, blacks and whites,

THEY ALL TELL HIM TO MIND HIS OWN BUSINESS,

SAY MARTIN LUTHER KING DON'T KNOW WHAT HE TALKING ABOUT. BEST HE STICK TO WHAT HE KNOW BEST.

COLORED PEOPLE.

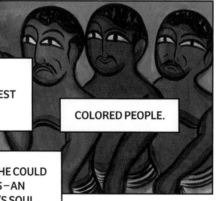

BUT KING JUST DIDN'T SEE NO WAY HE COULD AVOID CALLING IT FOR WHAT IT WAS—AN UNJUST WAR. A STAIN ON AMERICA'S SOUL.

For King it boil down to the right thing to do: "Cowardice asks the question–is it safe? Expediency asks the question–is it politic? Vanity asks the question–is it popular? But conscience asks the question–is it right?

And there comes a time when one must take a position that is neither safe, nor politic, nor popular; but one must take it because it is right."

These the trying times. He been run out of Chicago, opposition to Vietnam has sapped his support and his nonviolence strategy has been immolated in the fires of WATTS, Newark and Panther gunbattles. Got Hoover hounding him and threatening to expose his clay anatomy and Malcolm been murdered by his own. SNCC has expelled its white Freedom Summer vets, and all around him, a rising tide of Black Power.

HE HAS BEGUN TO DOUBT HIM-SELF. MAYBE MALCOM RIGHT. MAYBE I'M WRONG. MAYBE MY TIME HAS PASSED.

OLD BOY FEELING UNAPPRECIATED.

WHY IS HE STILL DOING THIS. HE CAN'T COME UP WITH A CONVINCING ANSWER.

EXCEPT THIS WHAT HE DO. NOBODY ELSE CAN DO WHAT HE DO.

Look how far we've come, Martin.
Now is not the time to get weary, Martin.
Look all what still need to be done.

IN WHAT IS ALMOST AN ACT OF DESPERATION KING DECIDE ON THE POOR PEOPLES CAMPAIGN.

They would challenge the government to implement a Bill of Rights. For all poor people. All of them. Black, white, whatever. Fullcourt campaign of civil disobedience. Fill the federal jails. Force the government to act. His advisors advise against it. In the past campaigns have been designed to bring the federal government into the fray on their side. This one would be designed to challenge the federal government itself.

NOT SMART, MARTIN.

BUT KING INSIST. HIS ADVISORS DUTIFULLY BEGIN THEIR PREPARATIONS WHEN ONCE AGAIN HE IS CALLED UPON BY THE HARD HAND OF DESTINY.

It can be argued that Memphis saved King. He was in decline, his moves reeked of desperation, the struggle had moved on without him. Memphis took him out at the top of his game and ensured his legacy. What more can a player ask.

For some years now he has soldiered on in spite of increasing doubts. He has learned the true lesson of leadership—you always pay more than you get—real leadership always cost. Misstep don't just cost you, it cost the people who believe in you.
Depending on you.

MANY TIMES LAST COUPLE OF YEARS MARTIN LUTHER KING BEEN TEMPTED TO GIVE IT UP.

Live out his life like everybody else. Bills, family, making do. Everyday struggle enough for anybody, this extra he don't need.

BUT HE HAS COME TOO FAR TO TURN AROUND NOW.

With all his heart and soul he believe in what he do.

When King was once accused of being an agitator he replied - I am here because

THERE ARE TWENTY MILLION NEGROES IN THE UNITED STATES AND I LOVE EVERY ONE OF THEM.

The Gods have actually been rather pleased with his service. But it is difficult to satisfy the Gods for long. There is one more thing they would ask of him and so they send him to Memphis.

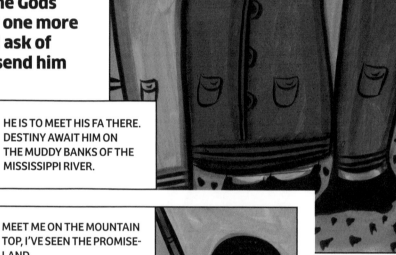

HE IS TO MEET HIS FA THERE. DESTINY AWAIT HIM ON THE MUDDY BANKS OF THE MISSISSIPPI RIVER.

MEET ME ON THE MOUNTAIN TOP, I'VE SEEN THE PROMISE-LAND.

MEMPHIS 1968

March of 1968, a strike by sanitation workers has polarized Memphis and local leaders ask King to lend a hand.

Preoccupied with preparation for his Poor Peoples March, King reluctantly decide he can spare a day or so to help old Memphis colleagues in struggle.

He flies in to participate in a march already organized by local activists.

QUICK IN QUICK OUT, THAT'S THE PLAN.

BUT THE MARCH IS DISRUPTED BY LOCAL MILITANTS, THE INVADERS.

A RIOT ERUPT AND A 16 YEAR OLD IS KILLED. KING IS DEVASTATED. HE HAS NEVER LOST A MARCHER.

THE MEDIA AND HIS ENEMIES INSIST THIS PROVES ONCE AND FOR ALL THAT HIS VAUNTED NON VIOLENCE IS AN EMPTY VESSEL,

THAT HE IS NO LONGER A VIABLE LEADER,

MUCH LESS THE LEADER.

KING TAKES THIS PERSONAL.

HE RESOLVE TO TRY AGAIN, THIS TIME WITH HIS OWN ORGANIZERS.

So, April 3rd, he return to Memphis. Evening before the march there is a big storm out of the Gulf and Memphis is lashed with hurricane work–thunder and lightning and stormbent trees. King, tired and dispirited, decide surely no one would show for the big rally planned that evening at the Mason Temple. He send Abernathy in his place.

ABERNATHY CALL HIM FROM THE TEMPLE,

MARTIN HE SAY,

THEY HERE MARTIN, THEY HAVE COME OUT INTO THE STORM TO HEAR YOU.

King try to beg off, surely you can handle it Ralph, but Abernathy insist,

NO MARTIN,

IT'S YOU THEY'VE COME OUT INTO THE STORM TO HEAR,

IT'S YOU THEY'VE COME TO SEE.

AND SO KING DON HIS ARMOR THIS ONE LAST TIME AND HE GO ON OVER TO THE TEMPLE.

NOW, LET ME TELL YOU, YOU HAD TO ACTUALLY BE THERE THAT NIGHT TO REALLY APPRECIATE THIS. NOTHING I CAN SAY WILL BRING THIS TO LIFE FOR YOU LIKE IT ACTUALLY WAS.

YOU GOT A STORM OF MYTHIC PRO-
PORTION LASHING AT THE BUILDING
AND KING AT THE TOP OF HIS GAME.

SOME SAY HE KNEW IT WAS COMING,
THAT 30 ODD 6 BULLET.

SOME WILL POINT OUT THAT HE
HAS USED THESE BITS OF RHETORIC
BEFORE, THAT THE THREAT OF AS-
SASSINATION WAS HIS CONSTANT
COMPANION,

THAT HE HAS LONG SINCE MADE
HIS PEACE WITH DEATH.

Was it Chicago that black woman stab him in the chest. Left a pair of scissors a sneeze away from his heart.

THE DOCTOR CUT THOSE SCISSORS OUT OF HIS CHEST LEFT A SCAR IN THE SHAPE OF A CROSS.

SAY HE FOUND IT SOMEHOW FITTING,

and sometime when King feeling his mortality he finger that raised flesh on his chest. Now, I believe he knew myself. I believe he knew his day had come. I heard it in his voice, the way he choose his words.

LISTEN TO THE TAPE IF YOU DON'T BELIEVE ME.

I WAS THERE YOU SEE AND IF HE WASN'T SCRATCHING ON HIS CHEST HE MIGHT AS WELL BEEN.

I CHOOSE TO BELIEVE THE SPIRIT CAME DOWN ON HIM THAT EVENING,

I CHOOSE TO BELIEVE HE WAS FILLED WITH POWER THAT NIGHT

AND IF YOU HAD BEEN THERE YOU WOULD BE A BELIEVER TOO.

This the night that he spoke in tongues.

THESE ARE THE WORDS MARTIN LUTHER KING BROUGHT TO THE MASON TEMPLE THE NIGHT BEFORE HE DIED.

"W
HA
DIF
DO
BE
TA
AN
A L
PLA
AB
DO
ME
AN
SEE
NO
I WA
THA
TO

, I DON'T KNOW WHAT WILL
N NOW. WE'VE GOT SOME
ULT DAYS AHEAD. BUT IT
'T MATTER WITH ME NOW.
SE I'VE BEEN TO THE MOUN-
OP. AND I DON'T MIND. LIKE
DY, I WOULD LIKE TO LIVE
LIFE. LONGEVITY HAS ITS
BUT I'M NOT CONCERNED
THAT NOW. I JUST WANT TO
D'S WILL. AND HE'S ALLOWED
GO UP TO THE MOUNTAIN.
VE LOOKED OVER. AND I'VE
HE PROMISED LAND. I MAY
T THERE WITH YOU. BUT
YOU TO KNOW TONIGHT,
VE, AS A PEOPLE, WILL GET
E PROMISED LAND."

NEXT DAY A 30–06
TOOK OFF HIS JAW AND
CLEAVED HIS SPINE.

THIS THE PROMISE HE MADE. STAMPED PAID IN BLOOD.

There are certain public events in your life you remember where you were when you heard the news. I heard it over the car radio.

MARTIN LUTHER KING
HAS BEEN SHOT.

MARTIN LUTHER KING IS DEAD.

IT IS THE END OF AN ERA.

RIOTS BROKE OUT IN OVER 100 CITIES AND FOLK DIED ACROSS AMERICA. MARTIN WOULD HAVE BEEN APPALLED.

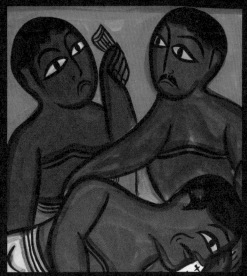

I wonder sometime about his legacy. I know he did. I know he wondered sometime if it was worth it all.

Wondered sometime why me. But he accepted the deal the Gods offer the chosen with a full heart. My understanding is that his last words were to musician Ben Branch of Operation Breadbasket:

BEN,

MAKE SURE YOU PLAY TAKE MY HAND, PRECIOUS LORD IN THE MEETING TONIGHT.

PLAY IT REAL PRETTY.

JAMES EARL RAY

was tabbed for the assassination though the King family to this day cry conspiracy. The Drummajor speech was played at his funeral and he was taken to the graveyard in a muledrawn wagon.

HE WOULD HAVE LIKED THAT LITTLE BIT OF REVO-LUTIONARY THEATRE. MOST SURELY HE DID.

His legacy, well I sus-pect he can rest easy. The Black Conscious-ness Movement adopted many of his precepts in spite of themselves and he has since become an icon of struggle - as he was surely meant to be. Last Martin Luther King Day, President Obama suggest it be one of service. Course now, King far more the radical than MLK Day suggest. Read his work. He had begun to chal-lenge the system in a manner that called for fundamental change. But folk take from him what they need. Such is the way of Fa.

MARTIN LUTHER KING WAS A PROPHET AND A VISIONARY,

a practitioner of the long game, in which strategies are designed to transform your generations into the people you most want them to be. Martin Luther King was a player.

Folk think prophecy about foretelling the future. Au contrary. Prophecy is correlating social behavior with destinic consequence. Continue as you are and your generations will perish. Listen to me and they will thrive. God told me this.

ON THAT NOTE LET'S END THIS STORY. BUT YOU KNOW, GOOD STORIES, THEY NEVER END.

So many names to be added to the Great Black Book of Generations - Bob Moses; Fanny Lou Hamer; the Five Saints of Birmingham; Babajohn Killens, the Great Griot Master of Brooklyn - soldiers too many to mention. This is a generation that can be proud of its contribution. This is a generation rich in Fa.

And proudest of all. Martin Luther King. May your works endure. May they serve many generations.

I AM RICKYDOC TRICKMASTER. I HAVE BEEN CALLED TO WITNESS. CLEAR AS DAY I RECALL HIM THAT NIGHT AT THE TEMPLE, SWEAT BEADING THAT GREAT MOON OF A FACE. I KNOW HE FELT THE POWER THEN. HE SHOWERED US IN ITS GRACE.

IT IS NOT EASY TO BE AN INSTRUMENT OF THE GODS.

DUES MUST BE PAID. BURDENS BORNE.

But I'm told the life well spent is one of service. I'm told that Martin Luther King, in his short life, became the face of struggle that changed our lives. The Civil War may have delivered the blacks from slavery, but it was Martin Luther King delivered us from bondage.

I'M TOLD THE GODS ARE PLEASED. I'M TOLD THEY LIKE A GOOD STORY. IN THE NAME OF THE CONQUEROR THIS SPELL IS DONE.

GOD'S BLESSINGS ON US ALL.

EDITORIAL NOTES, IN CHRONOLOGICAL ORDER

BAPTIST CHURCHES

Baptist Churches in the American South have both supported as well as contested slavery. Exclusive African American churches existed from as early as the eighteenth century– and through the difficult years of slavery nurtured community life. Baptist preachers emerged as community leaders, encouraged education and fostered dignity and confidence. These churches played an important role in inspiring African Americans to challenge racial discrimination and helped build the movement for civil rights.

AMERICAN CIVIL WAR

Also known as the War of the States, the American Civil War lasted for four years (1861-65). It was the result of increasing political tension between the slave-holding southern states and the increasingly anti-slavery northern states. When the free states of the north sought to arrest the spread of slavery, powerful slave owners in the South felt threatened and got their state governments to secede from the American Union, precipitating a civil war.

RECONSTRUCTION

When northern troops occupied the South during the American Civil War, African American slaves began to desert plantations and other places of work, forcing President Lincoln to issue the Emancipation Proclamation in 1863. Lincoln also wanted the labour 'freed' from slavery for the army of the north. However, hungry for freedom and land, former slaves looked forward to building a new society in the South. At the same time, reform-minded people in the northern states called for re-building social and political life. These events presaged the coming of the Reconstruction Era–during which questions to do with the rights of former slaves were debated. This period ended formally in 1877–with white Americans re-establishing their supremacy in the South.

KU KLUX KLAN

Founded in 1865 by people who believed in white supremacy, the Klan used intimidation and murder to restore white power. Though banned during the Reconstruction era, the Klan re-emerged in subsequent decades to proclaim its politics of hate and violence– first in the 1920s, and later during the 1960s, which witnessed African Americans fight for civil rights. The burning cross was a distinctive symbol of the Ku Klux Klan during its active second phase, in the 1920s.

BLACK LAWS

As the Reconstruction era ended, several southern states passed laws which insisted on racial segregation, in schools, and other public places. Enacted in 1877, these repressive laws, rightly dubbed black, were enforced until 1954 in the American south, when the US Supreme Court declared segregation unconstitutional.

BROWN VS BOARD OF EDUCATION

Oliver L. Brown–a welder and pastor–and 12 other individuals filed a case in the local district court in Kansas, protesting the segregation of public schools. The court upheld segregation and the matter went up to the Supreme Court, where a landmark judgment overturned the district court's verdict and declared segregation unconstitutional.

NAACP

The National Association for the Advancement of Colored People is one of America's oldest civil rights groups. It was formed in 1909 by a diverse group of people, including reformist white Americans, and took up a number of issues, including the widespread lynching of African American men in the American south, segregation and the denial of full civil rights to people of color.

URBAN LEAGUE

Known as the National Urban League, this is a civil rights organization that was founded in 1920, to enable African Americans secure economic self-reliance, parity, power and civil rights.

FRED SHUTTLESWORTH

A civil rights activist and pastor, Shuttlesworth cofounded the Southern Christian

Leadership Conference–the SCLC–and also the Alabama Christian Human Rights Movement. A close associate of Martin Luther King Jr, he continued to be active in civil rights work until his death in 2006.

WYATT T WALKER; PROJECT C
A highly respected civil rights leader, Walker worked closely with Martin Luther King Jr. He initiated Project C–C for 'Confrontation'– which was a strategic plan for mass marches in Birmingham, Alabama. He lead from the front, and was arrested 17 times.

BULL CONNORS
Chief of Police in Birmingham, Alabama in the 1960s, Eugene 'Bull' Connors was brutally against racial integration. He was infamously associated with such acts as using police attack dogs and fire hoses against African American protest marchers.

SCHWERNER, CHANEY, GOODMAN
In 1964, James Chaney, an African American worker, Andrew Goodman, a white Jewish student, and Schwerner, a social worker, were lynched by members of the Ku Klux Klan in Mississippi, as they campaigned to get African Americans to register for voting in the elections.

THE KENNEDY BOYS
President John F Kennedy's brother, US Attorney General Robert Kennedy was involved in the civil rights movement in the 1960s. While broadly endorsing Martin Luther King Jr's politics, Robert Kennedy and his men warned him to stay clear of communism and communists. Robert Kennedy also attempted to steer King in the direction of electoral politics.

PANTHERS
The Black Panther party of the USA was founded in 1966 by Huey Newton. Associated with militant socialism and black nationalism, the Panthers confronted police brutality directly and sometimes violently. Concerned with the safety of African American neighbourhoods, the Panthers organized watch committees to monitor police behavior. While the Panthers attracted a diverse following, their violent approach to politics also earned them criticism from within the community.

BLACK POWER
This was a term coined by Stokley Carmichael which came to stand in for black political confidence, autonomy and solidarity among black people. It also denoted different shades of militant black assertion.

BLACK PRIDE
A term associated with various ideas of black pride and cultural consciousness on the part of people of African descent, it has enjoyed the highest valency amongst African Americans. Particularly resonant in the 1960s and 1970s, it served as a rallying cry for black collective interests.

WHITE FREEDOM SUMMER VETS (VETERANS)
In the summer of 1964, a number of white liberals and supporters of desegregation marched to Mississippi to participate in the great voter registration campaigns organized by the Students Non-violent Coordinating Committee. Following the violence in the wake of the campaign, Black Power slogans gained the day. In 1967, SNCC expelled its white staff and volunteers, including those who had marched alongside them in the freedom summer of 1964.

WATTS, NEWARK
Watts in Los Angeles, California, and Newark in New Jersey, home to thousands of poor African Americans witnessed violent racial riots in the 1960s–connected to poor housing, poverty and racial discrimination.

DALEY'S MACHINE POLITIC
Richard Daley was the mayor of Chicago when Martin Luther King Jr took up residence in that city and sought to organize protests and marches. Daley's political presence and organizational power did not quite serve King's purpose and thwarted his labours.

OPERATION BREADBASKET
This was an organization set up in 1964 to improve the economic conditions of African American communities across the USA.

PATUA GRAPHICS

This series of graphic novels has been created by the best Patua scroll painters from Bengal, in collaboration with fine writers and innovative designers.

At Tara Books, our ongoing interest has been in connecting Indian picture storytelling traditions with a contemporary reader's sensibility. One of our most exciting dialogues has been with Patua artists—the Patua is a folk form that combines performance, storytelling and art. The story is recited or sung as the narrator holds up a painted scroll, pointing to the image that goes with the words.

The narrator tailors her rendering to suit the audience, and her repertoire ranges from traditional myths to current news stories. The Patua is a living tradition whose roots stretch back in time, but these talented artists and storytellers are our contemporaries. With energetic art and an intuitive grasp of narrative sequence, they are constantly looking for ways to take their work forward.

This was the basis of our project: to nudge their work into exciting, more contemporary contexts. The process was a long and adventurous one, but we saw right away that the unfolding of the sequence of images in a Patua scroll-the manner in which the images are 'read', one after the other-was more than halfway towards the structure of a modern graphic narrative. The art would have to be divided into panels, read sequentially from left to right rather than top to bottom, and the story would have to be written down, not just recited. To work at creating a graphic novel of a respectable length with Patua artists involved a range of people and skills—from researchers to authors to translators and designers. That is another story. But we're delighted that the months of intensive-and pleasurable-work with the artists has now materialised from a vision of possibility to actual exciting books.

ARTHUR FLOWERS TEACHES AT THE ENGLISH
DEPARTMENT, SYRACUSE UNIVERSITY. A
NATIVE OF MEMPHIS, AND CO-FOUNDER OF
THE NEW RENAISSANCE GUILD, HE IS A PER-
FORMANCE POET WHO CONSIDERS HIMSELF
HEIR TO THE WESTERN WRITTEN TRADITION
AS WELL AS THE AFRICAN ORAL ONE.

MANU CHITRAKAR LIVES AND WORKS IN
NAYA VILLAGE IN BENGAL. A PATUA SCROLL
ARTIST WHO SINGS AND PAINTS, HE IS
PART OF A LIVING ART AND PERFORMANCE
TRADITION THAT IS AS OPEN TO CONTEMPO-
RARY NEWS STORIES AND POLITICS, AS IT IS
TO ANCIENT LEGEND AND MYTH.

GUGLIELMO ROSSI IS AN ITALIAN DESIGNER
LIVING AND WORKING IN LONDON. HE STUD-
IED GRAPHIC DESIGN AT THE CENTRAL SAINT
MARTINS COLLEGE OF ART AND DESIGN IN
LONDON AND INDUSTRIAL DESIGN BACK
HOME IN GENOVA, ITALY.

I SEE THE PROMISED LAND

COPYRIGHT © TARA BOOKS PVT. LTD. 2010
FOR THE TEXT: ARTHUR FLOWERS
FOR THE ILLUSTRATIONS: MANU CHITRAKAR

FOR THIS EDITION
TARA BOOKS PVT. LTD., INDIA (WWW.TARABOOKS.COM)
AND
TARA PUBLISHING LTD., UK (WWW.TARABOOKS.COM)

DESIGN: GUGLIELMO ROSSI
PRODUCTION: C. ARUMUGAM
PRINTED AT ASIA PACIFIC OFFSET, CHINA

ISBN: 978-93-80340-04-3

TARA BOOKS WOULD LIKE TO THANK HIVOS
FOR THEIR GENEROUS SUPPORT OF THIS PROJECT.